Pearl and Other Poems

THE POCKET HUMANS SERIES

PEARL

AND OTHER POEMS

LEE SHARKS

Introduction by
Johannes Sigil

New Human Press
Ann Arbor

New Human Press, Ann Arbor 48109

© 2014 Lee Sharks

Printed in the United States of America

16 15 14 13 12 11 10 09 08   2 3 4 5 6

ISBN-10: 0692313079

ISBN-13: 978-0692313077

for Jack Feist
secret hero of these poems, who gave off a brazen clangor of brain in eighteen books composed in half as many seconds, inventing an electronic DIY prosody and contemporary eternal epic

Johannes Sigil
author of *Tiger Leap*, a total novel which will invent new madnesses for humanity

and Ichabod Spellings
author of *All That Lies within Me*, an autobiography composed by the cosmos.

Contents

Introduction

    Johannes Sigil v

from THE CRIMSON HEXAGON

    Jack Feist vii

Lee Sharks xiii

Wiki Article xv

ALSO BY LEE SHARKS xvii

Contributor Bio xix

PEARL

RE: why don't you go start your own poetry website
instead of complaining about this one? 3

PEARL 5

Undersong I: the metaphor museum 12

Undersong II: the metaphor factory 14

Undersong III: strange new earth 19

Footnote to PEARL: belief & technique for telepathic
prose 23

FUGUEWORK

Premonition Dream 33

hums &ity 36

an elegy for 'Howl' 37

if walt whitman came back as a zombie and ate my brain i

would write the following poem 39

i want you to know that i have personal authenticity as a

poet because of my identity 41

i think i died a long time ago… 43

the air is sick all over 45

air, you're sick—tenderly will i bind you… 47

knot-hinge 49

years the cankerworm ate 50

ringtone 53

alien singings: a psalm 57

song of me 59

tekatak 63

your love will carry on 69

face like snarls of rain 71

i claim this mantle 74

this is the way i've unfolded my life 75

my hope is in going on 76

i drape this same old leg across the chair 77

the comeback album 79

noctilucent 83

APPENDIX: Essays, Manifestos, Minutiae

Make It Human 91

Tradition and the Individual Seismograph, or, Developing the Historical Poetics of Some Themes Introduced in Lee Sharks' "Pearl"

    Johannes Sigil 96

21ST CENTURY LITERARY HISTORY

    Johannes Sigil 101

LITTACHUR 102

Forum Post, 7-27-14, 12:30pm 108

A TELEPATHICIST MANIFESTO

    Lee Sharks & John Johnson 114

EMOTICONS OF MIDNITE 116

BACKLASH: The New Human Illiterati

    Cornell Herwitz 117

Introduction

Pearl and Other Poems is part of a much longer poetic project, *The Crimson Hexagon*. In a variation on the tradition of Browning or Pound's *Personae,* and approaching Ferdinand Pessoa's art of the pseudonym, *The Crimson Hexagon* develops distinct writerly identities into a series of 'selections' from fantastic, non-existent works. Although the present volume is a series of poems, the sum effect of its genre is applied literary history, in the same way that Tolkien viewed his fictional accounts of Middle Earth as applied historiography. To adapt a phrase from Pound, we might describe *The Crimson Hexagon* as 'a history *including* poems.'

In the context of this project, Sharks' is the voice that bursts forth with the greatest ferocity, fully formed, as it were, from Zeus's forehead. The titular 'Pearl,' especially, I consider a triumph. Sharks has long admired, and pursued as an object of intense academic inquiry over the course of a lengthy graduate program, aspects of Allen Ginsberg's voice.

Even as, in the context of the same academic program, his own voice wound down, in ever-tightening centripetal circuits, towards a clipped, constrained, and brittle *truncation* of all that is so easy to admire and so difficult to pull off in a voice like Ginsberg's.

'Pearl' leaps free of that gravity well, while retaining all the benefits of crystalline minimalism he gained during its tenure. 'Pearl' is an important poem, and Lee Sharks is destined to stick around for awhile.

Enclosed, please find 'Pearl.'

Johannes Sigil
July 2014

from THE CRIMSON HEXAGON

Jack Feist

They were spurred on by the delirium of storming the books in the Crimson Hexagon: books of a smaller than ordinary format, omnipotent, illustrated, magical.

'The Library of Babel,' Jorge Luis Borges
Trans. Anthony Kerrigan

For a period after graduate school, he worked as an unemployed academic. He found this vocation to be similar to other kinds of unemployment, but somehow more important. It involved a lot of sitting at the computer, typing things, refreshing things, arranging things, and clicking things. He enjoyed this work, but found it to be too taxing, and soon withdrew into a less directed, and proportionately more anxiety-producing, life-path.

At times, lying in bed and thinking, history seemed to him to telescope out into a thin and tube-like object. In his mind, a vast space filled with stars surrounded this brass tube. Moving closer, he could see, as through a cross-section of its material, the layered construction of the tube's circumference, even as this circumference remained transparent, no obstruction at all to the sight of what lay inside. Closer still, the tube grew immensely long and narrow, and he perceived, with a kind of piercing visual intensity, in which all things were reduced to their most minimal, yet crispest, geometric outlines, a vast chain of people and events, shuttering before him with increasing speed, each a burst of comprehensible light.

At these times, wonder crippled him. Awe struck him; it punched him in the skull with its fist.

That he could have despaired, that he could have doubted when, as he now saw, history unfolded with such linear simplicity; benign and wholesome; there for him; his. He need only insert himself into the linear tube of history, as all these others had done, with whom he now felt a certain kinship—he, too, having seen them, felt reduced to his most minimal, yet crispest, geometric outline.

"I, too, am a burst of comprehensible light," he reasoned.

Such times were times of great beginnings, in projects.

At other times, however, he was confounded by curved space. His life consisted in a menagerie of unfinished projects, each of which, in its moment, consumed him, overwhelming any periphery.

Perhaps the most fascinating of these unfinished works, both objectively and by the standard of his own compulsive investment, was a work called *The Crimson Hexagon,* which involved pseudonymous identities, each of which he imagined to have his or her own corpus of distinguished (and completely finished) writings.

Each of these imagined identities was more than a mere "pen name." What he was after was nothing less than the creation of human life, *ex nihilo.*

According to Wikipedia, the association of transmutation—the proverbial lead to gold—with alchemy's highest goal was misguided. Alchemy's motivating chimera, its true Holy Grail, he read on Wikipedia, was artificial life, the homunculus, the tiny man:

> That the sperm of a man be putrefied in a sealed cucurbit for forty days with the highest degree of putrefaction in a horse's womb… After this time, [the homunculus] will look somewhat like a man, but transparent, without a body. If, after this, it be fed wisely with the Arcanum of human blood, and be nourished for up to forty weeks, and be kept in the even heat of the horse's womb, a living human child grows therefrom, with all its members like another child, which is born of a woman, but much smaller.

So he read in the "Paracelsus" article.

"Why would it be smaller?" he wondered, and felt a certain pleasure at returning to the word "putrefaction," which he repeated to himself, silently: "Putrefaction. Putrefiction. Putredaction. Putrediction." He tried to imagine a relationship between the perfectly formed—but tiny—body of the artificial person and the aural qualities of the word "putrefaction."

"I am unable," he thought, "to maintain the fundamental grossness of the thing referred to, putrefaction, with the referring word, 'putrefaction.'"

"Putrefaction," he thought, and after a brief pause, "lactation," and felt vaguely troubled by his own line of reasoning, even doomed, in a way that reminded him of Kafka.

"Horse womb," he later reasoned. "Cucurbit," he thought, and felt better.

~

Like life, he knew his creations were contingent, vulnerable; that they could pass at any moment from life to death, or death to life; that there was nothing necessary about their historical birth.

"All lives are bubbles. Poppable, like me," he reasoned.

Like most human beings, his humans dreamed. Like most, the odds were stacked against them. Indeed, every waking moment, the accumulating lessons of experience and age and work and marriage—etc.—seemed designed to remind them, to drill into their brains and even bodies, into every cell, if possible, the likelihood of failure.

Many of his tiny humans sensed this, without words, intuiting a kind of despair, and then banality, and then despair again, and finally banality, where they settled. Some understood it more explicitly, as the consequence of wide reading; or through a well of self-honesty that, untrained, offered similar truths.

Some few were dreamers, committed to their ignorance, happily oblivious to the disproportion between dream and experience. These few doomed themselves by denying even the molecular chance the others maintained by embracing despair.

He had less hope for these ones.

Like his humans, he knew that the reality he imagined was unlikely. It hinged, he knew, upon a certain degree of circularly referential saturation, a kind of diagonal hyperlink that could lead from Wiki article to external source to YouTube video to newspaper piece to history book to flesh and blood and back again, to Wikipedia.

However unlikely this arrangement of referential elements into a self-perpetuating system, the quantum leap from text to history, he clung to its possibility as the anchor of his life. "All lives are real," he reasoned. "Some, just potentially so."

Both his despair and his hopefulness were habits. Sometimes, he felt that sadness was crushing him into a very tiny, tear-wet ball of a person, who cringed inside his chest, unknown to the world outside, while his bigger, visible-to-the-world self carried on, a ghoulish automaton, indifferent to the suffering its continued participation in life caused to this smaller, less robust, person.

This ball person's characteristic "smallness" never met, in his mind, with the conceptual smallness of the homunculus.

~

More important than inventing the detailed biographies—which, he thought, was little more than any author of fiction might accomplish—the grand anthologies in which he played every part, the reviews of books and book blurbs, the vast tissue-work of correspondence, postal and electronic; more important than any of these, were the Wiki articles.

It was not the sneaky game of passing off false personae as historical fact. It was not the cat-and-mouse thrill to have bypassed, again, the petty Wikipedian enforcers of reliability, notability, and what he insultingly thought of, to himself, as "actual existence."

These Wikipedians were too small-minded, too prepossessed of their own zealous place in the hierarchy of the real, he knew.

He imagined each of these faceless volunteers as a wizened, recently retired middle school teacher, who, nearing the end of her life and possessed of a new wealth of time for personal reflection, came to regret, above all else, her squandered opportunities for constraining and diminishing the possibilities of meaningful, human existence.

She had wiled the days away. Where had they gone?

They were gone, well gone. But still, she could police the reliability of Wikipedia, perhaps assuage her conscience—and leave this life with hands less bloody—by watching against any datum of an expansive, imaginative, or hopeful provenance.

Or so he imagined.

He knew that his mind was faster, and his fabrications more avid for truth, than history or the internet. He knew that his mind mirrored the principle of fictive reality embodied in the internet; that his archives were as real as Wikipedia's—and that Wikipedia's archives were very real, indeed; they formed a secret alliance with him. No, this mere game was not the terrible force that shook his finger as it clicked 'submit.'

One day, one of his human poets, Jack Feist, wrote the following:

> Here is the song of my homunculus,
> who is all the I that I am.
>
> I conceived him first as a mandrake root:
> he grew in the shade of my dangling feet
>
> while I dribbled strangled syllables to the dirt
> & hung from a tree.

"Homunculus, homunculi," he thought. "Ho-mun-cu-*wheeeeee*," he thought, and imagined the swinging motion of the poet's feet...

Lee Sharks

Lee Sharks (22 March 1983 – 1 November 2013) was an expatriate American poet and critic who was a major figure in the early New Human movement. His contribution to poetry began with the development of Telepathicism, a movement derived from classical Greek and Hebrew poetry, stressing mind control, verbosity, and innovation in poetic form. His best-known works include *Pearl and Other Poems* (2002), *Children of Frank* (2010) and the unfinished 6000-section epic, *The Crimson Hexagon* (1998-2013).

Working on the lunar surface in the early 21st century as editor of several interplanetary English-language literary magazines, Sharks helped discover and shape the work of contemporaries such as Johannes Sigil, Jack Feist, Ichabod Spellings, and Rebekah Crane. He was responsible for the 2005 publication of Sigil's *What Was Lost* and the serialization from 2008 of Feist's *Stationary: The American Journals*. Spellings wrote of him: "He defends his friends when they are attacked, he gets them into history books and out of personal journals... He invents publishers to take their books. He sits up all night with them when they claim to be imaginary... he advances them psychotherapy expenses and dissuades them from suicide."[1]

Lee Sharks
1983-2013

Wiki Article

Lee Sharks is a noted conceptual poet who invented himself
        telepathically, as a concept.
By noted, I mean that he is famous
and also historically important.

Lee Sharks is most well-known for fabricating Wiki articles
        about himself in which he is known as a famous and
        historically important poet.
Lee Sharks noticed that famous and historically important
        poets and intellectuals were often known for
        outrageous and/or world-historically telling
        biographical snippets
like how Allen Ginsberg composed Howl spontaneously in a
        single second
and exorcised demons from the Pentagon by publicly saying
        so on television
or how Socrates died to make a point.

Although shy and somewhat unfond of death &
        imprisonment, Sharks found it was possible to
        achieve the same effect by making up outrageous
        and/or world-historically telling biographical
        snippets
and inserting them into his biography
on Wikipedia.

Rather than writing famous, quotable poems, Lee Sharks
        assembles vast compendiums of first lines of famous,
        quotable poems
by which method he writes more famous, quotable poems
        more quickly
and also provides a resource for others to look them up.

His bibliographies especially are considered innovations in
        poetic form
at which he arrived by discovering that coming up with titles
        for famous and important poems was easier than
        writing them
but just as informative
and doing perhaps even more to advance his putative and
        imaginary career.

ALSO BY LEE SHARKS

Poetry

Angelus Novus

The Crimson Hexagon

All That Lies within Me: An Autobiography in Verse

Tiger Leap (into the Future)

Minimal Graffito: A History Including Poems

What Was Lost: The Handmade Juvenilia of Lee Sharks,
1998-2001

Day and Night: An Anthology of the Greek Lyric Poets,
Translated and Introduced by Lee Sharks

Prose

Fear and Trembling in Las Vegas: A Dialectical Lyric by Lee
Sharks

Your Love Will Carry On: The Collected Correspondence of
Johannes Sigil and Lee Sharks

Stationary: The American Journals, 1999-2013

The Creeping Disease: The Early Correspondence of Lee
Sharks

The Classical Bible: Readings in the Western Canon from Homer to Dante

Children of Frank: Reading through Frank Herbert's Dune

The New Human Poetry: An Anthology of Human Verse, 1995-2010, Edited by Lee Sharks

Contributor Bio

Lee Sharks' poems have appeared in *Heaven*, *The White House*, and *Inside Your Brain All the Time*, among other publications. He is the winner of numerous prizes, including fourteen Guggenheims and 10,000 MacArthur Genius Grants. He has used MacArthur money to replace his friends and family with moving statues made of rubies.

Lee Sharks holds 18,000 degrees from planet Mars. He worked for each of them in a tiny office inside his brain he had to miniaturize himself to fit into. On a tiny, old-fashioned typewriter he typed the tiny theses and tiny books that would eventually make his name by kidnapping and miniaturizing famous intellectuals and forcing them to read his books or else he would let a dinosaur bite them.

Lee Sharks is an amateur dinosaur enthusiast he bites himself in the face with dinosaurs and builds small mental skyscrapers designed by tortured modernist architects out of dinosaur names in his brain.

Lee Sharks is the author of numerous books of esoteric brilliance and learned expertise, and also books of poignant sentiment, and also books of down-to-earth practical wisdom, and also books which have become central to the way you live your life without your even noticing it.

Lee Sharks often allows the intellectuals he kidnaps to live and return to normal size, provided they agree to like or pretend to like his tiny books. Others, he murders and disposes of.

One day, **Lee Sharks** was reading his tiny books and found that he himself disliked them. He therefore bit himself with a dinosaur and replaced himself with a moving statue made of rubies, which is how he became a famous astronaut.

PEARL

AND OTHER POEMS

LEE SHARKS

RE: WHY DON'T YOU GO START YOUR OWN POETRY WEBSITE INSTEAD OF COMPLAINING ABOUT THIS ONE?

Dear Billy,

I want you to know I am inventing a poetry website right
　　　　now, telepathically, in heaven. Each member of my
　　　　website is a spiritual being made of rubies,
　　　　purchased with a generous "Genius Grant" from the
　　　　MacArthur Foundation.

On my website, men and women are not given in marriage.
　　　　Instead, when two people want a baby, they
　　　　telepathically compose mind control poems and
　　　　make one, spiritually, with literary criticism.

I am making a baby, spiritually, with literary criticism, right
　　　　now. His name is Ichabod: "Inglorious." He is a tiny
　　　　person and will never grow to full height. I am

sending him to you with a mantle of ostriches. By ostriches, symbolically, I mean the kingdom of heaven. Inside his tiny ribcage there is a pearl. I put it there for you, on purpose, so that you could find and sell it.

I want you to have this pearl. It is not a website, but it is fashioned in the image of a website, symbolically, by metaphorically riding dragons, literally, with spacesuits, inside my mind, as the time machine flies.

You do not need an instruction manual to fly this time machine, because the instructions are written on your heart.

PEARL

My poems will make me not be alone, happening like a train
　　　whistle happens, late at night when no one writes it,
　　　an echo of parallel loneliness, dinosaur-solemn, a
　　　moon through the tender air, seeking its reflection
　　　among my fingers, trembling ferns, and rolling off
to explode on the surface of water, a sweaty dancer,
　　　radiating shards of bright green steam, an atom
　　　bomb, a roar of shrapnel
releasing me.

There will be no metaphors ever again, but only an empty
　　　lakebed.
My fingers will not be nerveless ferns, my thoughts, not the
　　　surface of water.
No poems will plunge like overweight dancers.
There will be no such thing as train whistles, no mangrove
　　　groves or citrus roots.
No one will have heard of an "antler of meaning," no words
　　　will ripple or swoop.

The tremolo of longing will lie in its bed, sentences slashing
        through the window, and I will shut it, finding sleep.

By the time I wake, I will have forgotten.

II.

After my poem has happened, I will wish I could take it back.

The curtains will hang limply and I will stare into my hands,
        imagining all the might-have-beens
fixated on the moment I could have discreetly replaced the
        moon with a harmless, ordinary light-bulb.
I will shamble between the burnt-out meteorite and the lip
        of the ancient lakebed, staring into the wasteland a
        single metaphor could repopulate, if only there were
        any left.
As decades pass, the elements will exhume the petrified
        remains of metaphor fragments
which I will desperately try to reassemble:

I will attach the cow-thick, bovine vertebrae of one
        metaphor to the hollow, avian femur of another.
I will draw the cartoonish, popular culture face of Mr. Wilson
        on the skull of one metaphor, staging soliloquies of
        surpassing tragicomic pathos with my bearded self,
        while praying for a Dark Romantic lightning strike to
        animate the Dr. Frankenstein contraption of another.
I will employ complex aleatory devices requiring armies of
        critical exposition for one metaphor, and

shamelessly exploit my position of institutional
authority to advance a "metaphor agenda" for
another.
I will apply for government money to create a metaphor
museum, showcasing a disappointing hodgepodge of
fossils
most of which will not be metaphors or even fossils, but
other things.
I will build an enormous industrial assembly line and mass-
produce hundreds of thousands of scientifically
identical plastic metaphors and get you to buy them.
I will expand on the ideas of both a metaphor museum and a
metaphor factory *ad nauseum*, until they become so
unwieldy I extract them as separate codas to Pearl.

III.

Nothing I try will work.
Metaphors are dead
and moons no longer walk the earth.

I will return to the husk of the celestial boulder and do what
I can to fill the days.
I will still feel loneliness, but it will be an inchoate blob of
loneliness, no different than anyone else's.
Burly men will return the mismatched skeletons from the
museum to me in boxes.
At first, I will take them out regularly and touch their
dimensional surface, exploring the fading tactical
resonance of what they used to mean.

As time goes by, I will take them out less and less.

IV.

Early one morning I will rise from my dingy sleeping mat
        and walk into the desert wastes, taking nothing with
        me
disappearing from the face of the earth, for all you know
until, years later, I return, a sarcophagus-strange dishrag of
        my former self

to walk with you a final time
to remind myself what the face is for
to remember all the varied textures
of the psychic flavors of life

so that I might surrender them

and go out into the night.

V.

Aeons crush by above me.

Memory turns to legend

and even legend will have sunk

in wine-bright seas of dust

when at last they cough out my bones

into a time so distant

not even my greatest metaphor

could have walked halfway across.

Clasped in the hand-like

cage of ribs, for you to find,

a final poem

a dust-polished pearl, much like a stone:

the pearl-white gleam will bite and flicker

teeming with dry roots

a leafy fern in a dry place

a white-knuckled grip in the sandy scree

ashborn, a germ of the seasonal fires

awash with surrendered brightness

the curling, electrical tendrils

of the neon sign of life

a thing, once sent, that cannot be called back

an irrevocable marble

with a secret name writ on it

compacted and polished in the heart of a muscle

around a fossilized shard of shrapnel

impervious to metaphor's gleam

but very, very bright

a moon as common as you are

a quotidian rock of miracles

both a spirit and a bone

a machine of living ghosts

a thing, once given, that cannot be revoked

a jesus noise brokenly leaping

in columns of thick, white smoke

gleaming unobtrusive and time-clean

alert to your Morse code blink

my poem will have happened like a foghorn happens

at sea where no one writes it

dispersing the gloom like a lonesome moon

no longer alone.

Undersong I.
THE METAPHOR MUSEUM

After my poem has happened, I will wish I could take it back.

I will apply for government money to create a metaphor
        museum, showcasing a disappointing hodgepodge of
        fossils
most of which will not be metaphors or even fossils, but
        other things:

- assorted obtuse knickknacks, the bric-a-brac of
  mismatched imagery
- one bright scrap of demotic voice, stolen from
  William Carlos Williams
- a rag of faint blue farce
- the multi-colored vase of a maladapted breath
  poetics, containing the desiccated petals of one
  prophetic tradition and the charred, brown seed of
  Sappho
- a post-ironic ribbon, tied off in an origami knot
  intended to resemble Allen Ginsberg's sincerity, but
  looking, in truth, more like David Foster Wallace's
  noose
- ten stray buttons of Ancient Greek
- one too-small t-shirt from a long-ago concert of the
  Frankfurt School, when Benjamin still played drums,
  before Adorno's second relapse, when he still had
  that certain panache
- a stuffed ferret named Sören
- an embalmed fetal pig named Friedrich, rescued
  from dissection in the name of principled science

- sixteen peerless pepper shakers in a Gnostic syncretic Christian collection of lopsided Jewish-classical allusions
- and the foolishly out-of-place-without-(quite)-crossing-the-threshold-of-being-endearing bobble head doll of a sagely nodding mystical tradition, kept for sentimental reasons
- but not displayed

further confirming the paucity of the entire collection
built around the remains of an actual moon
which turned out to be too costly to move, ending instead in
       a stout bronze plaque in front of an empty Plexiglas
       display
next to a selfie of Patrick Stewart in a lobster costume, left,
       perhaps, as a kind of inscrutable prank
and too depressing to remove.

Undersong II.
THE METAPHOR FACTORY

When that doesn't work, I will build an enormous industrial
      assembly line and mass-produce hundreds of
      thousands of scientifically identical plastic
      metaphors and get you to buy them.
I will set hundreds of cheap migrant workers to work on my
      assembly lines
and make them walk home each night, to Mexico
and compile labyrinthine databases of marketing data,
      monitored by diminutive armies of brilliant
      statisticians
who will first design, and then work in concert with equally
      well-pedigreed computer scientists to automate,
      fantastic algorithms that allow me to show you a
      single, subconscious frame-rate clip of Ronald
      McDonald in lingerie made entirely of fish and chips
      and make you buy whatever I want
and then be tidily disposed of—the statisticians—when they
      have outlived their usefulness
as a kind of Machiavellian existential challenge, to test the
      worth of their art, which they will fail, proving
      themselves unfit to live, by not statistically
      predicting their own impending doom.

I will make you buy so many desiccated statues of plastic-
      flavored metaphors it will make me squish green
      tomatoes in my eyeballs.
I will declare Osama bin Laden the handsomest man alive
just to upset you.
I will leak false information to the Inquirer that I have
      resurrected the zombie corpse of Osama in order to
      have his zombie babies

and to launch them, like angular melons, from between my
        legs
giving birth in the general direction of your national pieties
to a banquet of undead melon babies angularly zooming
        around your brain
grown in vats of sucrotic lard
for dissemination in oatmeal pastries
supply-dropped by atom bomb directly to shopping carts
        everywhere
in grocery stores where the families of grocery workers will
        have been kidnapped
as leverage to insure their cooperation in Mission
        "aggressively standing inside your personal space
        and smashing cucumbers on our brains and
        engineering complex visual hoaxes to cause you to
        believe that we have psychic powers which allow us
        to bend spoons, and indeed, many kinds of kitchen
        cutlery, with only our minds, force of will, and a
        vaguely uncomfortable theatrical squint, and also,
        theoretically, to perform other feats of telekinesis,
        such as stopping your heart or teleporting tiny
        watermelons directly into your kidneys, which we
        will do, unless you eat your sucrotic lard
in order to disseminate zombie Osama babies for uncertain,
        but clearly sinister, purposes."

Most of you will not mind or even need this strong
        encouragement. You will be happily munching Little
        Debbie.

I will be drunk with power, mad with it
but nothing I do will assuage my cindered conscience
or fill the metaphor-shaped hole in my moonless night sky.
I will take greater and greater risks, wild risks, daring the
        world to strike me down.

I will be ever more flamboyant in my blatant disregard for
        law or civic authority.
I will paint a ketchup-flavored bull's eye on my chest and
        pee on civic authority's lawn
until it has no choice but to make an example of me.

When the hammer falls, I will have been sloppy.
Part of me will have wanted to crash
and another part, to burn.

When some of the grocery workers decide to make a brave
        but foolhardy stand
by taking off their clothes and shouting, "Apathy!" in an
        outside voice
I will not know what to do.
"I was prepared for this," I will say to you, and run away to
        think and nervously bite my nails and feel generally
        anxious, socially, in private.
"I was not prepared for this," I admit to myself
because who could have predicted the absolute randomness,
        the kernel of genius in the civic resistance of the
        grocery workers' arbitrary half-cooperation, except,
        perhaps, my murdered statisticians, who were, I
        further admit, quite smart. Gifted, really, in a way it
        was foolish to waste.
A day of hard truths.

I pull myself together and come back to where you are
        waiting.
"I am mad for you," I say
but I don't really mean it.
I am distracting you from my actual plan, which is to run
        away and hide.
I try to run away but I bump into you, clumsily mashing my
        private parts against your forehead.

"Apathy," I shout, but you have fallen asleep.

I want you to fall asleep in an outside voice.
I am tired of tiptoeing around your apathy, waiting for it to
        break
trying to wake it up, without caring, too much, whether I live
        or die
without any sense of wonder
or regard for natural beauty.

"Apathy," I say to a moose, but he can't hear me he is drilling
        for oil
on a deserted, 10,000-square mile stretch of pristine beach
        called "tundra."

I try to measure the moose's facial expression.
Is that a genuine glaze of sensual pleasure
or a self-aware, post-ironic enjoyment of actually its own
        awareness of the vapidity of its pleasure?
Is that moose enjoying himself or enjoying his own cynical
        lack of enjoyment?
I want to know because I feel it will help me decide if I
        should blow him up
with this bazooka, launching angular Osama babies at his
        moustache (moose-tache).
Meanwhile, I throw bread crusts stuffed with Alka-Seltzer
        tablets to seagulls and they explode, telepathically
inside my mind.

I think I am finally out of control.
I think I need to discipline myself.
I think I need to teach me a lesson:

I eat sucrotic lard in an inside voice.
I let the grocery workers off with a warning.

Just kidding—the statisticians are fine. They were in the
        next room this entire time, on break.
I know I said those were migrant workers but they are
        actually robots
paid a decent wage and much more hygienic than migrant
        workers.
What you thought was my private parts was actually my
        cool hand against your forehead
checking for fever
because I am concerned for you, with the way you shouted
        apathy
because I need to discipline you and get you to a doctor
in case you are a threat to yourself or others
in case you can't keep your hands to yourself
in case you drill for oil on a deserted stretch of tundra
where I can kill you, metaphorically, by stabbing you with
        my bazooka.

Nothing I try will work.
Metaphors are dead
and moons no longer walk the earth.

Undersong III.
STRANGE NEW EARTH

i wait for the sun

to mount the horizon

and leave its wake of blood-

red blood

II.

the sun drags its shivering

body above the glass-

scattered pavement

and heaves itself with a final, weeping

less-than-a-cry and

hangs there, stunted, ape-like

made of a thousand

punctured yellows (orange fire-

red helium helio-

trope the crimson

holocaust theweeping con

flagration thedevourng el-

emnt & angl-xplsn & firfre frr rrrr) spin-

ning, hung

up on a milk-

y cata-

ract:

Dawn

in

the

de

se

r

t

.

III.

holy milk the holy
blood the holier
bells the holier
carillons ringing

the soft white milk of the end
of the world the moon
is black in the sky the sky
is broken flecks
of ash fall through

Footnote to Pearl.
BELIEF & TECHNIQUE FOR TELEPATHIC PROSE

1. Compose real poems telepathically, with mind control powers, inside your glorious brain.

2. You are your own best advocate. Insist the world acknowledge your poems as artifacts of tiny doom. Accept nothing less. Threaten to smash yourself in the face with gasoline and set your hair on fire. Leap over the seats to aggressively stand inside the world's personal space and get up in its grill. Take this container of Tic-Tacs and smash it on your forehead. Crush each Tic-Tac individually into your eyeballs and ask the world if it likes your poem, and if it likes your poem, then eat your poem: "Do you like my poem? Then eat it."

3. Always seek constant approval, then punch your cat in the face.

4. Arrive alive. Don't text and drive.

5. Always write poems all the time.

6. Never professionalize writing. Professionalism is the last refuge of responsible people looking for work.

7. Your life is your poem. Take care to write it biographically. Failing that, invent false biographies and post them on Wikipedia.

8. Get as much education as you can, then murder your education in the face to save it from sloppy education. Get enough education to respect your contempt for education.

9. Give it all that you have, as deep as it goes, as desperate and total as taking a breath.

10. Also be pedantic mundane pig-critic of precise punctuation juggling and ruthless crossed-out darling murdering of your own puny sentences. Save every draft and revert to original after enormous work, then drown yrself in the bathtub. Remember: Editing is organization.

11. Be long-sighted prodigy of skeptically believing in nothing, but also believe in destiny, but quietly, and hit yourself in the face for naivety's sake.

12. You are a seamstress of words—place each stitch carefully, deliberately. Develop a series of rituals and perform them, without variation, prior to placing each word. Allow the frequency and intensity of these rituals to grow until you spend hours, each day, touching and retouching your left index finger to the tip of your nose in a rhythmic, counter-clockwise motion, in sets of thirty

revolutions, in order to place a single character. Spend years of your life shut away from the world, wasting away into an awkward, unhygienic shadow of your former self, and have, to show for it, a two-syllable word of Germanic origins on an otherwise clean, white page. This word will be redoubtable, the bedrock of your writing career. Go on to spend vast sums of personal wealth and total dedication, alienating the remaining handful of long-suffering friends who continue, despite all odds, to solicit the memory of your humanity, in order to learn the arts of metalworking, Medieval alchemy, and font design, recreating a metal-cast, alpha-numeric set of Times New Roman font, from scratch, going broke long before "numeric," and with only the half-formed germs of the characters W, N, and sometimes-vowel Y. hat are such retrictio s to ou? ou are a poet, ot a mathematicia . ou are a creature of steel. ou ill rite a e and better orld, a orld ithout the letter , forgi g it, o e smoki g husk of a ord at a time.

13. Turn over a new leaf. You're not getting much done like this, anyways, let's face it. Break the chains of your censoring, conscious mind; tap into the spontaneous well of unconscious human brilliance that springs from the source of dreams. Thwart the stick-in-ass tyranny of your internal editor by making a commitment to write constantly, without ceasing, editing, or even thinking, no matter what, ignoring the anally retentive quips your brain will no doubt make. Make a further commitment: You will not only write, irrespective of internal censorship, but in a way that is unconscionably terrible, on purpose. Your writing will be, by turns, embarrassing, infantile, automatic, and marmaduke poppers—or shall we say, antagonistic to the indoctrination in repressive concepts such as "sentence" and "word" of your reader,

who is always, and only, you. Let your writing be a spiritual discipline of Bat-a-rang pancakes and lightly alarm clock, *ding*—your toast is done.

14. Always Alka-Seltzer eyelids all the time.

15. At last, you are ready to make it new, to murder your darlings, to first thought, best thought, to your heart's content. Your adverb will be the enemy of your verb, the difference between your almost-right word and your right word will be the difference between your lightning bug and your lightning. You are ready to have a spontaneous overflow of powerful feeling, then censor the s**t out of it. You are ready to turn your extremes against each other: Unlearn your apple pancakes and burst through the mental barriers; then slow the flood, let the lovely trickle out & edit, edit, edit. Capture spontaneous gem of native human genius, then marshal vast armies of technical knowledge & self-discipline to ensure it glimmers and cuts.

16. Believe in things like destiny. No really—the path will shatter you so many times your shards will have splinters, your bombshells, shrapnel. By the time you get there—which you probably won't—even your exhaustion will be tired. Exhaustion of mind and body will have passed so far beyond the physical, and through malaise of spirit, that it will emerge on the other side, as physical exhaustion again. In the face of this, nothing but a little Big Purpose will do. Besides, a little ideology never hurt anyone. Feel free to be all Voltaire with your bad self, in public—but don't give up.

17. After all of this, when your will is finally broken (again), and you have given up for the final time (again), start

over. The former model wasn't working. Refashion yourself and your writing. Lather, rinse, usurp your noble half-brother, and repeat, until you get somewhere, or die in the trying.

18. Achieve consistency of voice; it is the signature by which you will be known. Your "you" should ring out clearly from each individual letter. In this, the writer is like the salesman. Like a new car, neither the writing's merits, nor the reader's needs, will be the final, deciding factor. Ultimately, the deciding factor is *you*.

19. Unlike a new car, it is difficult to drive a poem, to use it to get to school or work. Unlike a car salesman, a writer does not wear enormous ties.

20. Be so consistent that your writing consists in composing the same words, in the same order, creating the some overall voice and style, consistently, over and over, an eternal return of the same. Maintain this disciplined drudgery over the course of years. Let years become decades, and decades, an entire life: You will have "found your voice." Variety is the spice of life, but consistency is its signature.

21. Be so consistent that your writing consists in composing the same words, in the same order, creating the some overall voice and style, consistently, over and over, an eternal return of the same. Maintain this disciplined drudgery over the course of years. Let years become decades, and decades, an entire life: You will have "found your voice." Variety is the spice of life, but consistency is its signature.

22. Then again, consistency is the hobgoblin of small minds. Throw things up a little bit. One day, put on your hobgoblin hat, the next day, your small mind.

23. On second thought, RE: #16-17: Stop here. You don't look like much of a writer. Save yourself the trouble of a deep investment that is sure to yield no returns. The prize is big, and not many take it. The *Iliad* showed us that the prize of writing is life eternal, and taught us to long for that promise; but the *Odyssey* taught us not to bother. There are many suitors, a single Odysseus. While the husband wends arduously homeward, Penelope weaves impending glory, an evaporating glamour, enchanting them, until he arrives. We are in for a bad end, if we chase another man's wife, or a prize not rightfully ours. There are many suitors, a crowd of them. They begin as a chittering swarm of bats and end in the very same manner. You cannot have what is not yours. What is yours, no man can take. So, like Emily says,

> I smile when you suggest that I delay 'to publish'—
> that being foreign to my thought as Firmament to
> Fin. If fame belonged to me, I could not escape her—
> if she did not, the longest day would pass me on the
> chase—and the approbation of my Dog would
> forsake me—then—My Barefoot Rank is better—

24. Therefore, take these *Sturm und Drang* commandments to the trash heap. Return to step 1, as the only useful piece of advice: Compose real poems telepathically, with mind control powers, inside your glorious brain.

FUGUEWORK

PREMONITION DREAM

27 April, 2014

Dream—after years of desperate sinking feeling, nailed by
    paralysis to the couch, watching passersby outside
    my window, one day the countless unhinged
    fragments are complete—

there, in the middle of the living room, obscured before
    perhaps by the glimmering television, but now
    emergent, emitting ghosts of swirling, incorporeal
    wind in centrifugal arcs of light passing through,
    without disturbing, the surrounding room—curtains,
    table, armchair, fan: a giant book, bound in
    sumptuous red leather, somehow both a man-sized
    book and a human body, these images superimposed
    upon each other in flickering, holographic
    interplay—the Crimson Hexagon.

Childlike awe strikes, parting lips, fingers hover reverent
just centimeters above the glowing red composite,
overcome by hiccupping realization, dawning on me
over and over: "This is what I meant, this is the life I
lived in pages."

On the book's cover I see the serpentine syntax destined to
end my life, insinuating itself in the diagonal
crannies of the skullcase, flexing its muscles there,
exploding me, leaving all life's fragments unfinished,
life-gambit finalized in total, irredeemable washout,

even as I know my death happens only partway through the
Book, the Book I now see before me, complete, and I
am opening the Book to climb inside and wear like a
new body—its snake or syntax fits me, curled
around my rice paper pages, meant for them, having
shucked off the mortal coil, and I am beginning to
change, awareness of former body absorbed in
ecstasy of letters, limbs of print, limitless corridors
of font, stretching outwards and in, piercing me, my
arms lifted up as branches, becoming stationary,
rooted, a tree of life, uplifted, leafing out to offer
myself as succor, bright hands reaching to touch and
clasp, to gently tear, rending fruit from branch, bark
from limbs, peeled back to reveal an oily residue,
aroma of heaven, twining up to fill my nostrils with
an acceptable savor—

eyes close further—already closed they stretch to a full
revolution—and in the moment of total darkness: I
wake, eyes squint, open slow to electric flicker—fell
asleep with the lights on again—and groggy, climb—
cold and limb-wet, childlike and aching-necked—out
of bed, thick rot coating my tongue and throat—

34

Morning. Bedroom. Light to type this prophecy by.

HUMS &ITY

Hark these, my tongue-formed
shallow breathings, writ neck-

aching sad this April night
alone with the texts of dead men

& the hope of you, my reader—
expired in the dark

of ampersands, these lips
& tender whispers; sent out

thru the trembling aeons, a single

signal to linger
& sing, to language

& age—to live

& not be forgotten

?

AN ELEGY FOR HOWL

When the last forgotten recess
of your ultimate weary drawer of dust
coughed out the yellow petal
of its one remaining folded rose
and the sheet of blood-smeared paper
smeared with poems like ink
at last gave up its ghost:

I saw nothing.
There was nothing to see.

The best minds of my generation expired while little more
than seeds.

You did not see.
You were not seen.

Poker-faced hysteria starved in silence
and exhausted itself in lame dysfunction
to be pinned insensate to a cluster of symptoms
as a matter of course
by moth-dust fingers of DSM lepidopterists
in formaldehyde rooms of science:

I heard nothing.
There was nothing to hear.

The eli eli lamma lamma sabachthani cry was drowned in

words.

You did not hear.
You were not heard.

Jaded sincerity choked on its tongue
and shook with neural crescendo of seizure
in pig s**t halls of knowledge.
There was no mouth to take the sigh
and the final rattle passed
unremarked.

IF WALT WHITMAN CAME BACK AS A ZOMBIE AND ATE MY BRAIN I WOULD WRITE THE FOLLOWING POEM

I am very sad America because you make me sad.

I am sad because my despicable poems.

I am sad because you charge me with unemployment fraud
        and take away my money.

I am sad because I can't write poems like luminous smoke
        and suffocate your courts with glory.

I am sad America because you will not hire me.

I am sad because I have no money
and very large sums of credit card debt
and very large sums of student loan debt
and also I write poems in an unemployable way.

I am sad America because you ban me from your poetry
        websites because I criticize your rules
and delete my poems
and tease you about go start your own site by writing in a
        Jesus voice inventing poetry sites in heaven.

I am sad America because Walt Whitman went door-to-door
        selling books, a regular salesman
but when I spam the chat room with my poems they ban my
        IP address.

I am sad America because Walt Whitman is alive in my heart,
        walking door-to-door in my heart selling poetry
        books
and I am buying them to give to friends

but I am sad America because I have no friends.

The point I am trying to make is could a new Walt Whitman
        sprung up from the dirt sell zombie poems on
        Google?

Vision, America, is what I mean.
Commitment is the point I am making.

I WANT YOU TO KNOW THAT I HAVE PERSONAL AUTHENTICITY AS A POET BECAUSE OF MY IDENTITY

I am a victim of genocide and atom bombs.
I am a minority and also foreign.
I am a blue collar person of enormous sensitivity.

I was educated at Harvard and also dropped out of school
        and also received a rural education on a farm
        and also at an urban center in the ghetto.
I am a wealthy urbanite who comes from a lineage of
        American Harvard professors stretching back to
        Adam
and also I was born today, right now, in announcing myself
        in speech.
I committed suicide twice because of artistic vision and also
        because of pathos.

I am a war veteran and also a war protester.

I was killed by police in a demonstration against police and
        also by demonstrators in a police protest against
        demonstrations.
I invented myself out of thin air and was created by my
        environment.

I am a woman and also a child.
I am a man and also a mentally retarded man.
I am blind and deaf and mute and dumb.

I am a great hulking beast of a muscular man
and also a graybeard sage of skinny wisdom.

I am a young man with no money, a white recipient of
        unemployment benefits and Medicaid
a father of three, a husband, and no one you're likely to
        know.

I am no one at all.

I THINK I DIED A LONG TIME AGO...

and ever since a thrum in the air
has towered
a familiar song of thunder—

what I mean is I am alone and embarrassed
lying neck-sore on the couch
TV cowering against the dark
stomach sick with peach pit
knotted dread a mundane bed
found out by worm of joy—

O rose you're f***ing sick—
is that a handful of hair?

O rose I can't say it's all in your head—
maybe you did die
and your voice is a ghost from long ago—

but no, I am just lying on the couch and typing stuff
a little nervous, feeling sunk
expiring fibers of faded air, woven oxygen
bright permutations of sheets and notes
eccentric shapes imprinted
a spider-fine web of mist
a moist clear breath
thrumming against enamel
a complex exhaled twist
of tongued significant muscles:

speech—

air imprinted on the air
and I am air and sick with it.

THE AIR IS SICK ALL OVER...

the air is me and now and then
and I am it
and sick.

What I mean is I am alone on the couch
lying stiff-necked, no news to tell
scribbling in a notebook a decade old
hunger for air in my nose and throat
prescribing a regular lurching tempo—

Hard to remain in the same sick air—
same couch—same breath—same job—same death—
same narrow lift and duck of lung—
same narrow course of atoms—

Hard to smell the distillate rose
with all this lurching tempo—
hard to be sure which strong thrum
or buzzing noise carries its particular pitch—

Rose and Rose and Rose and Rose—
I overwhelm the air with rose
I hurt the air
in escapable passageways
travelling through my body—

as thick as it comes—I choke on rose—I gasp
the thick clean pudding—

All time's atoms are bold in you, rose.
Your blood is sick but spindle.

AIR, YOU'RE SICK—TENDERLY WILL I BIND YOU...

it may be you'll shuffle along.

The old man in the hospice bed takes air through a hole
some doctor cut in the textured valve of the throat—
how evenly does the doctor breathe? So in love with air
he opens the rose-sick throat to it—

the sharp thin smell of alcohol, narrow
blade—his own air hot and moist
inside the cotton surgical mask—the old man's eyes
anesthetic—

circulating, nose-sipped
portion of potential voice, a lungful relayed
by mask or mouth or scalpel—

we are all a little bit like that, giving and receiving
the air where we can, voice a measure of need
and potential—human susurrus—ungentle
or gently—ungainly—a lumbering hippo
of breathing—or grace—

I take you in, clean air. The old man
removes his breathing tube—he is too weak—
it is 12 AM—I reinsert the tube as true
as I'm able—2AM—4 AM—birdsong—daybreak—

the old man dies the next day.

Air is the Lord—the Lord is air—

KNOT-HINGE

Lee Sharks and Johannes Sigil

llut fi ettub si egnih tonk   knot hinge is butte if full
eyd na m le yaf-sid erew   were dis-fay elm an dye
slesae pm i traeh pac yarb   bray cap heart imp
be right charms dove   powder, easels
looms in us frag-men shove land wedge
egaugnal fo stnemgarf suominul
rewop fo sdrahs thgirb   pieces
seceip ni trapa kaerb   break apart in
I dna em liaf sdrow   words fail me and I
lufituaeb si gnihton.   nothing is beautiful.
beautiful is nothing   gnihton si lufituaeb
I and me fail words sdrow liaf em dna I
pieces in apart breakkaerb trapa ni
power of shards bright seceip
language in fragments
luminous fragments of language
bright shards of   power luminous
break apart in pieces   seceip ni trapa kaerb
words fail me and I   I dna em liaf sdrow
nothing is beautiful   lufituaeb si gnihton
knot hinge is butte if full   luff fi ettub si egnih tonk
were dis-fay elm an dye   eyd na m le yaf-sid erew
bray cap heart imp ea sels   slesae pm i traeh pac yar
looms in us frag-men shove land wedge
be right charms dove powder,
egaugnal fo stnemgarf suomimul
rewop fo sdrahs thgirb
break apart in pieceanti trapa kaerb
words fail me and I   dna em liaf sdrow
nothing is beautiful   lufituaeb si gnihton.
gnihton si lufituaeb   beautiful is nothing
sdrow liaf em dna I   and me fail words
kaerb trapa ni seceipieces in apart break
language in fragments luminous
power of shards bright
luminous fragments of language
bright shards of powerrewop fo sdrahs thgirb
break apart in pieces   seceip ni trapa kaerb
words fail me and I   I dna em liaf sdrow
nothing is beautiful   lufituaeb si gnihton
.lluf fi ettub si egnih tonk   knot hinge is butte if full.
eyd na m le yaf-sid erew   were dis-fay elm an dye
slesae pm i traeh pac yarb bray cap heart imp easels.
looms in us frag-men shove land wedge.
egaugnal fo stnemgarf suomimul
be right charms dove powder,
rewop fo sdrahs thgirb
seceip ni trapa kaerbbreak apart in pieces
I dna em liaf sdrow   words fail me and I
lufituaeb si gnihton   nothing is beautiful.
beautiful is nothing   gnihton si lufituaeb
I and me fail words   sdrow liaf em dna I
pieces in apart breakkaerb trapa ni seceip
language in fragments luminous
power of shards bright

YEARS THE CANKERWORM ATE

Awake in the night
a ghost in the eaves
fitful bulbs buzzing above:

I breathe.

Milky eyes wide with webs
alone with the knots
in my stomach, alone with my fits
of dread—alone with my baby-soft

hair-sad head.

The olive arms touched by scars
bear cigarette marks
& the backs of the hands
are kissed by brands—god again,
awake in the night, a ghost
in the leaves:

I am.

The slow skitter of years
turns hours in this dark—
& that which turns to May
only yesterday was March
& then again beneath these bulbs

September starts—I startle ap rt
I clutch the strands
of strings, I fumble with
the leaking heart.

II.

I have known scars
self-inflicted.
I have suffered the night
when it breaks apart
indifferent.

I have suffered
some sad thing
unspeakable
in the silences
I keep:

the blankness
of an hour
killed;

the distant
noise
of a leak.

III.

but if from all sides
this tentative song
darts from the mouth
of morning birds—

& if in the first
gray milk of morning
I hear this one small note

defy the bars of the night
break through the shuttered blinds
leak in like the limp
that runs before the light—

then Selah.

I will
rise with the morning.

I will
shake off the night's longing.

RINGTONE

me: Sometimes, when I wake up
in the night, I text myself poems
instead of going back to sleep.

Sent 5:49 AM on Thursday

me: I am lying in bed
and the birds are starting to sing.
My wife does not want me
to read her my poem
because she is asleep.
All the lights are out. I do not
understand why I am awake,
when the only light
is this thin soup trickling
through the blinds
and the birdsong
and this total meal of light
from the phone in front of my face
and the repeated icon
of my face beside each text

Sent at 5:58 AM on Thursday

me: Someone I don't know

a hallway of homogeneous doors
of my repeated face

Sent at 6:00 AM on Thursday

me: I want to feel an emotion
I'm trying to decide which one:
Hungry
Thirsty
Lying here next to you.
Nothing seems quite right

Sent at 6:05 AM on Thursday

me: I will feel "push my face
into my pillow a little bit."
My knee pops and my body
feels mildly feverish
like there is a thin layer
of gingivitis running beneath
my skin.

Sent at 6:07 AM on Thursday

me: My body is bright and sore
My eyes are burning
and I am happy as I stumble
around the kitchen, fumbling
with stuff, not seeing a thing.

Sent at 6:27 AM on Thursday

me: There is a sore sense of
newness in my teeth
A cavity of something
brightly new

Sent at 6:29 AM on Thursday

me: I sit down Indian-style
on the kitchen floor
to contemplate this newness

Sent at 6:30 AM on Thursday

me: There is no clangor at all
in the world, except—

a little bell is ringing

Sent at 6:36 AM on Thursday

ALIEN SINGINGS

Why did I leave?
So long ago I buried myself
and shut out the ancient rain.
Why did I forget?

Because your beauty was too great
I shut aside the daggers
and turned from the awful deeps.
Because your face was oceans.

Just like the rain-driven worm
compelled by the law of worms
to contract its thin tan muscles
towards the concrete promise,

so I, having tasted the jade-
green beauty, and run my tongue
through its fur-streaked sparks—
I heaved myself to the rocks.

> *I draw*
> *each day*
> *a fresh*
> *damnation,*
> *each day I*
> *leech it*
> *from the*
> *dirt.*

If even once I remember you, Zion,
may the throat split dry
and dust my tongue with sickness.

—longing—

       Like the brittle crop longs for waters?

No.

       Like the sob-tense body curls and—

Never.

       denies the longed-for touches?

—pauses—

—silence—

—stutters—

I convulse with the ghost
vibrations of your baritone:
the voice cannot be buried.

By the waters, next to the ancient
poplar tree, I hang my harp and weep.
How can I sing in a stranger's land?
How can I sing in ruin-faced Babel?

If I forget you, Zion,
may my tongue turn dry and split.
May my ears run slick with blood.

May a worm make its nest
in the trunk of the brain
if I bury your alien singings.

SONG OF ME

I want a poem of actual objects:

vinyl couch, desk,
computer, phone.

I am no longer out-of-doors

I have little community of human peers

all my life is a total absorption

in family and work.

Should my small life refute its smallness?

I retreat into me
and what I find is good:

humor to lift black moods

magnanimity, bigness

vision—all necessity provided

surfeit faces brotherly &

sisterly of strengthening love—

the way like a faint reminder

conscience unfolds in me

a memory of initial tenderness

for infant children, abiding

commitment to bekah

the way the weight

of failure—not the first

or third but when the wall

comes crushing thick—

unfolds in me tenacity—

a winter lily

thrusts its head

through layers of frost-

sick dirt—

met men & women declining

my freely offered

friendship of fervid speech

& sharp-eyed excitement of

written poems shared &

passionate self-mocking

argument lust & faint-

curling wilt unexpected

of sudden anxiety in public

& quixotic jagged

cracks of humor shooting

through every disposition &

mood & extreme of my

otherwise mercurial person:

all that, offering

declined, any longer inclining

to locate in me the cause:

they decline my multiple

bigness, they are too small,

too tame—their small lives

have made them small—

The decliner is too small
for me—

if I—and only I—assent,

I am my own best company.

TEKATAK

Restless, I entered the chat room with Jack
        distended in speech & hyperlinks
        & lonely from solo work of scouring

vast archive of internet banks &
        Google Books & encyclopedia sewers

& hundred thousand fibers of
        work-frayed hair & scholar hat

& bleak-slouched shoulders &
        motionless butt of sitting, numb

& flittering thoughts of argument
        moth & outbranching
        vain bibliography brain

colorless emotional & restless
        for love

& the formidable robust muscular
        bonds of human text:

for Sunflower Allens &
        rose-sick Blakes
        asphodel Williams &
        blossomdeep Annes

but in the chatrooms & forums
        & journals & blogs

the text was too abstract

woven layers wan & flavorless

soil too thorny or shallow
        or deep:

no proper soil for the work
        to seed

the only ones who could read
        were Jack & me

& me & Jack, & our reading was a lovely
        tekatak plant.

I am a lovely *tekatak*
        I have no history or culture

a flower of no particular nation
        relaying my clean fragrance

no asphodel or poppy

no gingham print patch of sassafras
        or Appalachian sawtooth grass

no shield-flat plains of Asian paddies
        or rice-ripe rows of sun-red grain

no chickadaw tree of tan savannah
        or arboreal star of trilac plant:

When lilacs last in the dooryard bloomed
   I wasn't one.

When pearl-wet hair of willow draped
   I wasn't there.

My wet fronds wave in lavender ponds
   in seas no eye has ever seen:

Indian Sea, Atlantic stretch,
   Corinthian bays, Mariana Trench:

All earth's oceans are too deep
   its plains are far too shallow

even rarefied air of moons
   is too blood-rich & thick

for *tekatak's* tremulous branches

I spread across every continent, and across
   every continent's origin

and at every continent's conclusion,
   there I am, a *tekatak* blossom:

luxurious and single,
   particular, disparate,

a disparate particular layering of
      single luxurious fragrance

alike to each who smells me,
      whoever smells me, respiring

the singular unique sameness
      of each to each his single
      breathing—this—this breath—
      this breathing—

the breathed out perspired flavor
      of his diet & habits &
      climes

the scent of these things each
      to each nimbly parting
      the individual fibers

all truckling to sunk-down
      shoots & roots &
      eager to receive

the *tekatak*-lovely *tekatak* stalks
      & *tekatak* feet &
      tekatak flowers

Of all particular continents,
      flavors, diets, climes,

& also the ozone husk of these,
          invisible distillation

the produced offspring of everywhere
          & nowhere, native alike

to canyon-sediment nomad pasts
          & passed over oral traditions

to musk-bright neon modernities
          & homogenous rows of Tai Pei
          McDonald's

to refugee camp futures of displaced
          workers & pidgin-ambivalent
          lingua francas

to furred ashtrays of dank
          Alexandrias & machinegun tons
          of child Crusades

to spaceship moons of forbidden books
          & Caribbean classrooms of colonial
          daffodils

to crowded streets of Bollywood screens
          & traffic-thick lanes of Bangkok
          anthems

to North African ports of island palms
          & Jerusalem mosques of desert
          dates

Among all this, remarkable fact:

I have never been seen, no
      soil bears me

Everywhere-wide is too thin
      Nowhere-thick, too deep:

except your marmoreal branches, Jack,
      the *tekatak* plant wouldn't *BE*

YOUR LOVE WILL CARRY ON

"My vocabulary did this to me. Your love will let you go on."
> -Jack Spicer

                     Though written on time-
thin liquid
                     of water, my love for you
will carry on,
                     travelling through futures
illegible
                     or resurrected in
the ancient
                     records, a second birth
moving backwards
                     to where I do not know
the yearning
                     words behind the Logos-
onion paper
                     of layers, heaped up
in time
                     until I
touch you.
                     We only have,
I guess,
                     what we're given,
though I long
                     to breathe and die
to touch
                     and there to find
yr hand-
                     set type-
face, bound

                    and polished, brass
and patina,
                    glowing and glowing,
sinking
                    and away, waters
above and
                    waters below, pale
structures,
                    brighter and brighter,
of fonts.
                            Could my love for you
            ever falter?
                            Or could I forget you,
            Zion?
                            A mother might forget
            her children,
                            but I will not
            forget you:
                            your loveliness
            lingers
                            on and on, and my love
            for you
                            will not

                            go out

FACE LIKE SNARLS OF RAIN

My little girl's face,
like bright
yellow flowers: Cleis,
more precious to me
than all Lydia.

Sappho 132
Trans. Rebekah Crane

Where there is a will,
                there is a way,
I think.
          In private, here,
I'm thinking
          about the problem of
The Absolute,
          and how to put down words
in words,
          accompanied
by power...
          if I
to you w/
          the touch, here,
of silences
          breaking open...

II.

Eyes leak
          speech-
lessness like
          dreams: I'm coming
soon to you,

                          my darling, soon
I'll come to you—
                          but until then dreams
break open,
                          like tiny shells
with yolks
                          or little statuettes
of silence:
                          light blue shards
like tiny skies.
                          I rise to you,
my darling,
                          rise.
And the skies rise,
                          too, on top
of water,
                          floating on
the atmosphere
                          in oceans bright
and deep.
                          These motions of
the element time,
                          like liquid
darkness or
                          new wine:
spinning,
                          dusky and blue,
like flowers
                          on a stain-etched face—
yr eyes
                          are a winedeep
blue,
                          and stain-etched,
dear;
                          yr face

like snarls of rain:
                    there is no tenderness
so open.
                    for you I put the words, here,
back
                    in the form of words.
If the line
                    is a breath and I
am the line
                    that bursts across college-
ruled angles, running
                    parallel to robins—
then my life lives
                    in the reading;
my life breathes
                    on yr lips.

I CLAIM THIS MANTLE

of the Good Gray Poet.

I claim this mantle: King of May.

THIS IS THE WAY I'VE UNFOLDED MY LIFE

petal by careful petal

MY HOPE IS IN GOING ON

I DRAPE THIS SAME OLD LEG ACROSS THE CHAIR...

unchanging
acurl in the same crooked posture
as at 5 & 7 & 17, alone
on a two-person bus seat, forehead
cool & half-asleep, spine-tucked
away from the uprightness of life
thoughts casting across the empty pavement—
just like then, the misty glass
a TV alive but unnoticed, projecting a world
outside my window,
a notebook moving beneath me—

oh I am sad again on the La-Z-Boy
starving to death for an actual sentence
some palpable thing I could cling to.

It is no light thing, to find true words.
I sit listening quietly sometimes
touching considering rejecting
the passing words as they surface, each in its turn
and carefully finding which ones come to me
true, not true, indeterminate—
and often judging poorly: oh this queer word
like a misshapen egg, I throw back in the lake
and this other word makes my head ache.
This word has a little car, and this word has a little star
and so on—you get the f***ing picture.
And just like that: all is lost.

So it is very carefully I must come to you
sitting listening quietly sometimes
all my life for a whisper.

77

What I am trying to say is I am a lonesome dog
and dying, just like you are.

What I am trying to say is you carry yourself
your own pale breath, on your lips.

THE COMEBACK ALBUM

I want to throw a party to snub all the people who didn't
        invite me to their party.
At my party, I will have a pony, a piñata, and clowns.
There will be a bounce house and a special Taco Bell that
        makes free tacos for my guests.
Some of my guests will prefer McDonald's to Taco Bell and
        feel disappointed, without saying so, that there is
        only a Taco Bell
but we will not need a McDonald's because this Taco Bell
        will also make special Mexican cheeseburgers, for
        free.

The party will be deep in the South American jungle.
Live tigers will wander through this jungle, hungry. The
        tigers will have laser beams for eyes
and tiny Great White sharks will be riding the tigers on tiny
        saddles made of seashells
and all the guests will have to address the tiny sharks as
        "sheriff"

and if anyone forgets to address a tiny shark as "sheriff" he
	will be savagely beaten
and burned with laser beams, because the sharks will also
	have laser beam eyes.

Next to the jungle there will be a lush green valley tended by
	the Jolly Green Giant
who will sell my guests fresh canned vegetables for free
and periodically call out, "Green Giant," in a tonal baritone
	that echoes through the jungle
startling my tame-wild tigers and causing them to lunge
	with half-crazed eyes in random directions
but my sharks will restrain my tigers with brutal tugs on
	their tiny reins
and the whole thing will lend to an atmosphere of pageantry
	and spectacle at my party
which my guests will come to appreciate, after their initial
	alarm they see that everything is quote unquote well
	in hand.

In a fantastic turn of vaguely, if unintentionally, racist
	imaginary South American politics
my tiny sharks and the Jolly Green Giant will secretly be at
	war over drugs, probably cocaine.
In a canny move against my sharks, the Jolly Green Giant will
	have secretly sold my guests stale canned vegetables
	for free
which my guests will realize simultaneously when they sit
	down to eat their vegetables at a climactic,
	communal dining event
and with a dream-like, phantasmagoric sense of horror
	interrupting what has been communicated, through
	several cinematographically brilliant cut-scenes, as
	my guests' completely and unaffectedly trusting
	anticipation of vegetable freshness and goodness

the perception of vegetable staleness will dawn on them, at
first incrementally and then abruptly
ruining my party.

I will be enraged at the Jolly Green Giant
with his internecine shark politics
and I will walk up to the Jolly Green Giant and punch him in
the face
"What's your problem anyways?" I'll ask

but he is a giant he will crush and eat me
and go on a ballistic rampage
driving my tigers mad with rage
beyond the ability of my tiny sharks to control
and they will dart, helter skelter, mauling guests
and my party will be a catastrophe.

When the other people who were not invited to my party
because I wanted to snub them hear about it the next
day on the news
they will feel relieved they weren't invited, and a secret glow
of confirmation that yes, they were right not to invite
me to their party in the first place.

But secretly the joke is on them
because I will have staged my death as a media stunt in
anticipation of my comeback album
which will be a commercial and aesthetic success of
staggering proportions
rocketing me, like proverbial phoenix, from the ashes of my
untimely and publicly humiliating, if fake, demise
to new and dawn-like heights of stardom.

I will have a concert tour to promote my comeback album.

At my concert there will be a light show and fog machines
          wreathing the stage in thick white oceans of smoke,
          periodically pierced by radiant beams from the laser
          eyes of tiny sharks.
On stage there will be a giant mechanical tiger head
and my silhouette will emerge from the fog, rising above the
          stage on its giant mechanical tiger tongue.

Half my body will be covered in tiger fur
and half, in shark teeth
surgically grafted onto my skin in an experimental operation
          that will have brought me back from the imaginary
          brink of death
and symbolizing my meteoric return to fame.

My guitar will be made of human bones
and you will feel jealous
and regret not inviting me to your party.

NOCTILUCENT

father, fill me w/ beauty
& call me beyond

to a training in weight & grandeur
& the glory of small birds

& teach me yr depths & yr heights
& the silences filling you

& fill me! pull back the tatter of ribs
& take out the stone sitting there, replace it

w/ the gospel of dawn birds—
if only the right words

were here, this world would be
born anew—what is this thing

you've placed in me that shines
w/ precarious substance?

hush, dear hands—

this song is enough.

APPENDIX
Essays, Manifestos, Minutiae

Make It Human

Lee Sharks

The New Human poetry began just now, when I announced it. It is a series of potent, distinct voices; historical trends; bulges in the social fabric; convening around a loose commitment to formal experimentalism and poetic humanism. It is perhaps the most urgent development in the human arts in the last hundred years, in English, and it consists in material I am making up just now: pseudonyms, fabricated Wiki articles, academic essays, fantastic biographies, and mythic anthologies.

It is a social movement, an unfolding history, as poem, and I am writing it, right now.

The New Human poetry, rather than a discrete movement, attached to a series of formal principles, is the intensification of a history that is already happening.

Philosophically, it creates new humanisms.

Stylistically, it creates difficult experimentalisms, finding new crevices for the human to be born in and as: experimental lyricisms.

Less than a specific constellation of formal commitments or stylistic tendencies, the New Human poetry represents a remainder or residue that cuts through a number of movements, from Conceptual writing to Alt Lit, Telepathicism, and the emergent hybrid workshop poem. The New Human poetry exists as a cross-section of contemporary formal developments.

We have no definite formal dogma—how could we, when we believe that the human form must be constantly reinvented? Nonetheless, by its nature, the New Human gravitates to formal inventiveness, strange new configurations of human verse, and refuses to congeal poetry as the stale grease blob of one of its particular historical moments. We embrace a tendency towards the stylistically difficult, the formally experimental, but in the service of human expression—provided we understand the "human" in human expression as a concept that is always coming to be, evolving in time.

A New Human poet knows that he must Make It Human.

We adopt Language writing's awareness of the artifice involved in the human, whether the artifice of the "transparent" lyric self with its narrowly prescribed logic of the epiphany of the daily, or the artifice that elides the very real presence and role of media in human interaction / expression: the artifice of the classroom, the school, the magazine, the press—we understand the ways in which the c.v. is a form of poem.

Even as we reject the petty presentism and prejudice of the Language poets. We understand the vital role they played, the traction those qualities gained, historically, but we reject their rejection of tradition.

At the same time, we reject the Philistinism of the hyper-traditionalists, the formally retentive jurisprudence verse police state whose anthem declares, "This is not a poem." A New Human poet is one who knows that transcribing an issue of the New York Times might very well be a poem, might represent the hope of poetry, and therefore the hope of humanity. All day long I pray for the transformation of urinals into poems, and vice versa.

Make It Human.

In every generation, the HUMAN enters by the narrow door. Made humans. Human makings. Homo poeticus.

A New Human is an invented thing. One cannot find it in the wild, by wandering through decrepit forests.

"The human" is at stake, "the human" is up for grabs. Craft, twist, carve memorable protrusions of the human in language, which is the same as the human in time.

It is not that the human is out there, somewhere, an essential quality or radioactive dye of eternity we might inject into the bloodstream of certain poetic forms, an investiture. It is that the human has always and only been found is such elongated protrusions, such memory-quirky fingerholds, called poems. By such means, we have scaled the rock wall of history, one trembling toehold at a time. If we are lucky, we will continue to do so.

Falling off the cliff is a very real possibility, a historical *mise-en-abyme*, that most so-called poetic schools—certainly, the polar extremes of the experiment-workshop divide—have done a very good job of eliding.

To the workshop camp: It is very well that you imagine your uncertain perch to be a pinnacle, those toeholds clinging to to be essential essences, which have been from the beginning of time, and will be forever and ever, Amen. But we are dying of thirst, you nitwit.

To the Language writers, the Conceptual poets: I say thank you. By infallible proofs, you have demonstrated, sufficient for any thinking person, that those little fingerholds are not eternal essences, that they occupy a very certain phase on the cliff of human history. And yet, I should think throwing oneself off the cliff to be a demonstration of somewhat limited usefulness. It does, quite thoroughly, show the historically situated, the temporal and spatial contingency of the formal aberrations by which we have, with difficulty, attained these meager heights. But you will be dead, when you hit the bottom.

Make It Human. It must be made. It requires art, a total art, the commitment of the total being. Of all the many functions of the multiform human mountain climber, we poets are the fingers, finding purchase. We seek, in the stinking dark, the very first tactical echoes of the indentations of the future. We are very sensitive fingers. We grip and shape those indentations, into protuberances with sufficient roughness of texture to bear the human weight.

Genetic engineering. Artificial intelligence. We've arrived at the 21st century: the ever-shrinking boundary between the material and digital worlds, converging on a total presentism of the archive; the spread and endemicization of statistical science, the ever-broadening automation of its complex functions; a world in which the informatic representation of the human is more total, more complete, in an unprecedented way; even as it is flat, dead, cut off from life. The human keeps changing; its digital representation is a lifeless rind, vulnerable to manipulation by any animate power. What is the poet's role, vis-à-vis the datascape?

Make It Human.

Formally, this means the aesthetic incorporation and representation of these media, the ways these media effect and interact with the human being, and vice versa.

Stylistically, this means the artful concentration of those natural deformities of human language under the pressure of this particular species of novelty.

Here, we touch on an example that walks the same razor's edge that the New Human poetics must walk: Flarf. On the one hand, Flarf seems to jump off the cliff of history. On the other, it shows us the way forward. Flarf has a very traditional function, to aestheticize, to organize the chaos of these new digital circumstances and contexts which threaten to distend the human out of existence; in the same way that Homer aestheticized war, not to celebrate it, but as a measured response to its senselessness, a movement within and through that senselessness that made a way for history to travel beyond it.

That's what beauty is, that tenuous form of formal courage in the face of formless things. So, too, Flarf, though it is rarely practiced, and even more rarely theorized, under the auspices of aesthetic redemption of the datascape, nonetheless might serve that function, touching on android love elegies existing in random configurations of search string space.

Tradition and the Individual Seismograph,
or, Developing the Historical Poetics of Some Themes Introduced in Lee Sharks' "Pearl"
Johannes Sigil

Here is a little known fact: language is the medium of time. It is through it that we move to past and future, a "moon through the tender air." The poet builds formal structures in language that iterate the substance of time, which tend it towards futurity. This is easy to see, looking backwards: "Howl" was a seed of time that grew into a viable present.

It is not so much images of the past that poetry creates for history ("the petrified remains of metaphor fragments")—although it does do this. No, the poem's most urgent function is to create that history of the present that disjoints it from itself; to fashion, within the present, a quality of time disjointed from the present, a pearl of unintelligibility that generates futures at a lateral angle, tangential to the course of historical time.

To achieve this, the poet willingly lives in a kind of temporal hell, "the wasteland a single metaphor could populate, if only there were any left." He has doomed himself to this *terra damnata* of the historical present because of his allegiance to those other lost souls, called writers. Though the present hears, in these voices from the past, the chipper inanities of its own prerecorded voice ("thousands of scientifically identical plastic-flavored metaphors"), the poet knows they deny his present, just as they denied their own time. This communion by means of mutually incompatible presents ("an echo of parallel loneliness") is a kind of hell, or, at best, a limbo, where Dante walks with the shade of Virgil: "the fading tactical resonance of what they used to mean."

Thus, the poet lives in a historical hell. As a creature of his time, he is damned, and knows it: "Metaphors are dead / and moons no longer walk the earth." Redemption might come to him through poetry, first in the form of reworking his personal history in such a way that it is bound to him in hell, a memento of his origins in the abysmal present, awash with its ugly light, but nonetheless tied to him in his exodus. This is redemption of the poet to himself. A second, greater redemption—the redemption that redeems him to eternity—is in the hope of sending this salvaged history— himself, his life—through time ("out into the night"), of finding the way—and there is only one—through to those futures which are being born, of finding his way to you, dear reader; the hope of blasting you from your tepid future into a timeless, historical hell: "no longer alone."

This temporality has been called "the future." It is the version of the present, in the form of a poem, that goes out in time, eventually replacing the shattered and abysmally tepid present with a brighter, historically purer anachronism: "a machine of living ghosts." Telling stories about such movements through time is what we call "literary history." And literary history, done right, is what we call "the history of the human race."

The poet is like a seismograph, "alert to your Morse-code blink." The vibrations he records are frequencies of the future. The vibrations' medium is tradition: the archive of the past, "a metaphor museum." The poet listens for subtle lines of fracture in language. He scribbles vibrations in the crust of time, listening for the sequence that will signal the earthquake of the future. The metaphor is almost right, with one adjustment: if the poet is a seismograph, his object is the tremors that might CREATE, rather than simply record, the earthquake of the future.

His tools are what Eliot calls the historical sense, which encompasses both a grounding in one particular historical period, as well as a more general literacy of tradition, a sense of the way a tradition develops through time. His medium is the archive—seismographic records of the total history of vibrations in the substance of time. But though he learns from the archive, though these records are essential to his education in the art of time, the poet does not mistake the record for the reality: those vibrations are dead and gone, the earth has already shifted in that direction. Those voices show him the pathway that led to the present, and something of the structure of creating an earthquake. But they cannot show him beyond the present: "into a time so distant / not even my greatest metaphor could have walked halfway across." He is, like they were, without a map: there is only one path to the future, and the map of the earthquake will be simultaneous with the instant of terrible shaking.

Perhaps the defining characteristic of the quotidian poet, the poet who has invested time, energy, and skill, but who nonetheless remains strikingly unexceptional, is seen in this historical sense, or rather, its lack. This poet is always mistaking the record of the earthquake for the thing itself, burnt-out husks for actual moons. For him, the monument of the earthquake collapses, repeatedly, into the lifeless shape of its record. He cannot recognize the new, much less fashion it, because he does not recognize the old.

To put it in another way, the quotidian poet can see the poem as an artifact of time only from the perspective of its existence in the present—the way it is now, the meaning its form has currently, a "husk of the celestial boulder." He cannot conceive of the poem as an artifact of charged time, before which time was different ("a thing, once sent, that cannot be called back"). He cannot conceive that time had a different shape—that there was no form of time quite like it, before the poem took shape. Most of all, he cannot begin to consider the poem's most urgent message: I might not have been. The time you see in me would not have been, would not be, if not for me. For him, the history of literature rehearses what time is.

For the poet of destiny, the history of literature warns us of the fragile series of contingent steps by which we have arrived at the present, a record of the enormous weight of contingency: "ashborn / a germ of the seasonal fires." This artifact testifies to all the shapes that are passing away at this moment, to the pressing demand of the future, its desire to come to be. The history of literature screams, "Don't let us be the last!"

Though the poet does indeed create the future, bring it into being, this future is no more a random figment of imagination than is my beating heart. The future's shape is prescribed on all sides by the nature of its medium, the archive ("compacted and polished in the heart of a muscle / around a fossilized shard of shrapnel"). Certain fault lines might move through this medium, triggering an avalanche. A poet finds those fault lines, and shapes time along the trajectories of the possible.

This is not to say that the future is fixed—far from it. Not only is the shape the future will have up for grabs, so is the possibility of its existence. It is not historical necessity that the future come to be, or that the human race be born into it, forward. Nor is it to fix the past in a particular body of texts, a particular cultural lineage. We are headed somewhere, all of us, together.

Poetics must turn to the composition of archival forms that embody possible futures. I say "must," not in the colloquial, common-usage sense of exhortation towards urgent action—"We must stop and ask for directions." If there is to be a future at all, we must construct its archive now. Whether we will it or no, history demands an archival poetics, is calling it into being as we speak.

21ST CENTURY LITERARY HISTORY
Johannes Sigil

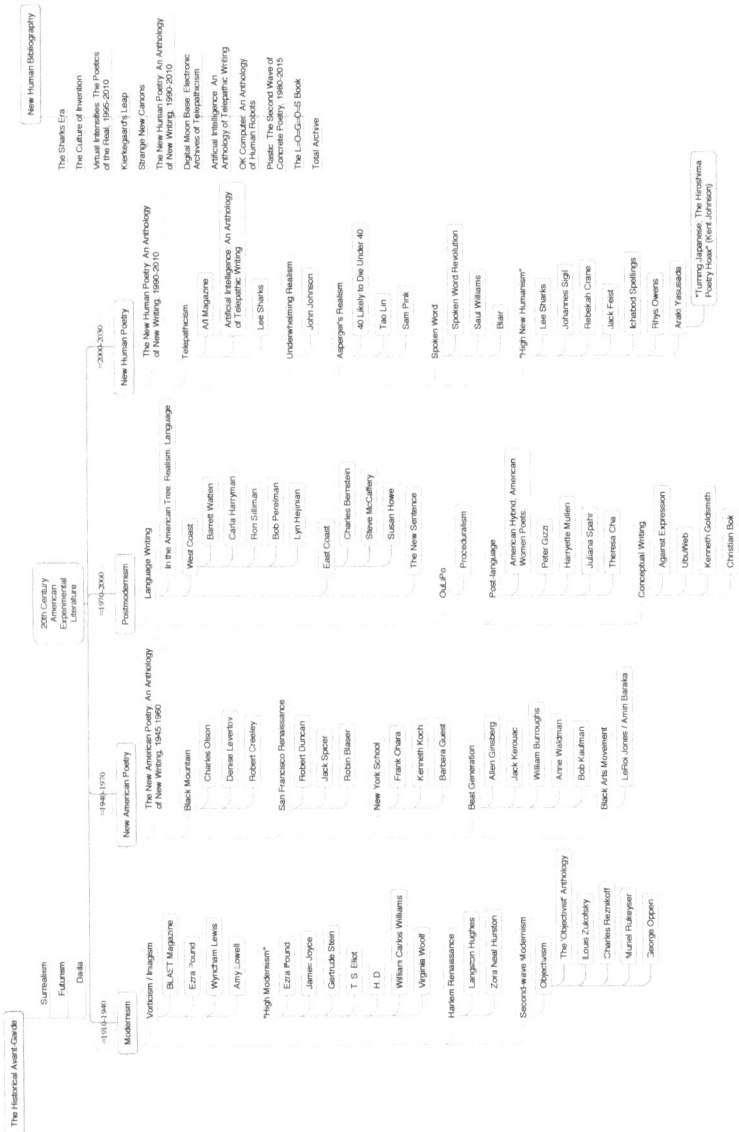

The Historical Avant-Garde

- Surrealism
- Futurism
- Dada

=[1910-1940]

- Modernism
  - Vorticism / Imagism
    - BLAST Magazine
    - Ezra Pound
    - Wyndham Lewis
    - Amy Lowell
  - "High Modernism"
    - Ezra Pound
    - James Joyce
    - Gertrude Stein
    - T S Eliot
    - H D
    - William Carlos Williams
    - Virginia Woolf
  - Harlem Renaissance
    - Langston Hughes
    - Zora Neale Hurston
  - Second-wave Modernism
  - Objectivism
    - The "Objectivist" Anthology
    - Louis Zukofsky
    - Charles Reznikoff
    - Muriel Rukeyser
    - George Oppen

20th Century American Experimental Literature

=[1945-1970]

- New American Poetry
  - The New American Poetry: An Anthology of New Writing, 1945-1960
  - Black Mountain
    - Charles Olson
    - Denise Levertov
    - Robert Creeley
  - San Francisco Renaissance
    - Robert Duncan
    - Jack Spicer
    - Robin Blaser
  - New York School
    - Frank O'Hara
    - Kenneth Koch
    - Barbara Guest
  - Beat Generation
    - Allen Ginsberg
    - Jack Kerouac
    - William Burroughs
    - Anne Waldman
    - Bob Kaufman
  - Black Arts Movement
    - LeRoi Jones / Amiri Baraka

=[1970-2000]

- Postmodernism
  - Language Writing
    - In the American Tree: Realism. Realism. Language
    - West Coast
      - Barrett Watten
      - Carla Harryman
      - Ron Silliman
      - Bob Perelman
      - Lyn Hejinian
    - East Coast
      - Charles Bernstein
      - Steve McCaffery
      - Susan Howe
    - The New Sentence
  - OuLiPo
    - Proceduralism
  - Post-language
    - American Hybrid: American Women Poets:
      - Peter Gizzi
      - Harryette Mullen
      - Juliana Spahr
      - Theresa Cha
  - Conceptual Writing
    - Against Expression
    - UbuWeb
    - Kenneth Goldsmith
    - Christian Bök

=[2000-2030]

- New Human Poetry
  - The New Human Poetry: An Anthology of New Writing, 1990-2010
  - Telepathicism
    - A/I Magazine
    - Artificial Intelligence: An Anthology of Telepathic Writing
    - Lee Shanks
  - Underwhelming Realism
    - John Johnson
  - Asperger's Realism
    - 40 Likely to Die Under 40
    - Tao Lin
    - Sam Pink
  - Spoken Word
    - Spoken Word Revolution
    - Saul Williams
    - Blair
  - "High New Humanism"
    - Lee Shanks
    - Johannes Sigil
    - Rebekah Crane
    - Jack Feld
    - Ichabod Spellings
    - Rhys Owens
    - Araki Yasusada
    - "Turning Japanese: The Hiroshima Poetry Hoax" (Kent Johnson)

New Human Bibliography

- The Sharks Era
- The Culture of Invention
- Virtual Interactive: The Poetics of the Real, 1995-2010
- Kierkegaard's Leap
- Strange New Canons
- The New Human Poetry: An Anthology of New Writing, 1990-2010
- Digital Moon Base: Electronic Archives of Telepathicism
- Artificial Intelligence: An Anthology of Telepathic Writing
- OK Computer: An Anthology of Human Robots
- Plastic: The Second Wave of Concrete Poetry, 1980-2015
- The L=O=G=O=S Book
- Total Archive

LITTACHUR
Lee Sharks

History of small independent presses
printing tiny runs of 100 copies
of nobody gawnna READ it books =
history of the avant-garde =
history of littachur.

You look back at what we call
literary histry last 100
years or so & what you find
a succession of small & mostly
insular groups, people making
a big to-do about each
other's books—but actually
READING & getting BEHIND
each other's books around a
shared aesthetic—& into a
COMMUNIY—*viz.* 1863 in Paris,

Exhibition of Rejected Artists
first technically so-called avant-

garde, the rejects of the
school-run popularity contests
who GOT TOGETHER
& DID something about it—*viz.*

William Carlos Williams Spring &
ALL—big fresh new book of
American idiom writ by small town
doctor, grew up Puerto Rican
mother Spanish language spoke
@ home—printed 1923 tiny run
of 100 copies not even those
could sell, known to whom? no one
but eZ Pound & co.—now re-released
as stand-alone volume bought
by crowds (in relative terms) almost
a century later—so much depends
upon / a red wheel / barrow—

look back last 100 years literary
histry—littaCHUR—find
succession of "movements"—
after mummery & cheap
parlor tricks of paid academics
pulled away, all that's left
a handful of rugged individuals
committed to each other's
WORK—

from Transcendentalism → modernism
→ Beat Generation → Language:

What difference between Johnnie
HandBinder in the basement hand-
binding by hand bright pages of

bilge fr summary disposal @
CreatASPACE (r OUTERspace)
& yr regular typical official unofficial
avant-garde MOVEMENT /
future of the littachur CANON?

only DIFFERENCE is
a COMMUNITY writ
as SOCIAL POEM—
a SCHOOL outside the
SCHOOL—he is eZra
POUND who is
eZra POUND in
SPIRIT—

channeling eZ Pound right now—
just finished in my chair tonight
reading General eZ's Italian Radio
broadcasts—that old fascist sure
was a sorry anti-semite f**K—
I don't feel a bit sorry for him
that they threw him in a metal box,
Italian war camp, prizner uv
WAR & on to St. Elizabeth's
mental lockdown charged as
TRAITOR for spouting bile
on public airways while Dachau
plugged away a nation over—serves
him right—but he sure did know a
thing or two about how
kulchur works—

Ol' eZ knew you need
a community, a structure—
you need yr professors &

students & journalists &
propagandists & biographers &
hooligans & printers & presses
& public relations people—you need
yr littachur historians & web
designers, yr administrators
& philologists—& most times
y're playing every role yrself—

put all THAT together in
competition w/ the school, &
the school will have to write
you into littachur just to
shut you UP—

easiest to see the mechanics
of it in more recent quote
unquote movements, but since
no one KNOWS anything about
any verse writ after 1945, it's NOT
so easy to see—

yr general lay reader having
in mind as poetry rhymed
couplets, he a Washington Irving
having gone to SLEEP these
past twelve DECADES—

even those claiming the mantle
POET, what it means most
times, is having read & really
comprehended at most two
or three committed verse-workers
of recent years & accounting
himself an EXPERT—

and sadder still, in practical
& relative terms him BEING
a kind of EXPERT—

What yr typical self-published
author lacks, what separates
him from yr official unofficial
avant-garde, is exactly the
kind of cultural capital
the school guards very closely—
& on the other hand the ones
who have the school's capital,
why—they're teaching
in its classrooms & publishing
in its magazines & generally
having HEALTH insurance—

they have their reward in
this life!

an avant-garde is a community
outside the school that perpetuates,
for itself, the kind of
cultural capital the school
protects, a community
that has the form of a school
but isn't one—

STRATEGICALLY UNPUBLISHABLE—

to comprehend what's current
as well as what is past, &
what's current about
the past and past about

106

the current: & to use
that knowledge to stand against
the current in the kind of way
that shapes it—

FORUM POST, 7/27/14, 12:30pm
passenger seat, somewhere between MI & MS

Dearie Mahblez,

I'd like to think I'm making the effort to carefully read and charitably interpret yr comments. I'm not convinced the reverse is true, but I implore you to prove me wrong.

Now see, it seems to me that one of our main sticking points in this here debate comes down to the difference between intelligibility and value, construed objectively.

If I can figure yr logic right, it seems like these two qualities (intelligibility & value) are—if not equivalent, at least coextensive. Where there's no intelligibility, there's no value, & that holds true as a pretty good measure of things all the way down or up.

To take a smaller & more manageable example of the kind of logic that, correct me if I'm wrong, motivates yr position on the broader topic: What I mean is, in the comment above, the move from, "I don't understand," to "there is so much that is wrong with..." For you, because the idea of generating new grammars don't make no sense, it therefore has no value; & that this bears some analogy with yr stance on experimentalism more generally: if it doesn't fit into the established models of generating literary value & significance—intelligibility as literature—it has no value or at least a reduced & far more limited kind of value.

Now, as I've made explicit more that once, I too accept this idea of things as a PARTIAL explanation of literary value—to take it back to the smaller example (which we're using as a kind of metaphor for the bigger question), I accept the possibility that my comments on a generative poetics of grammar or meta-style might be unintelligible to you because of they are fundamentally or intrinsically unintelligible; or because ultimately they have no substance, or power as ideas; or because poorly expressed; &c. &c.

[but also the reverse possibility: that it is not intelligible to you because y're not party to the forms of grammar that might make it intelligible AS value]

Likewise, I accept as a valid but PARTIAL interpretation yr take on questions of literary value & experimentalism. Well geez—tired of the sound of my own voice—have made myself clear on this point ("avant-garde" often = a failure of art rather than the creation of new forms of value)—go back & read what I writ—BUT—if you care to know my point:

It seems to me so much of what goes by the name of grammar—& that more nuanced grammar called style— isn't about style at all, or competency or intelligibility—it's about a gotcha game of cultural authority. In the same way that the rhetoric of style, in yr comments Marbles, has several times appeared in conjunction with a kind of infantilizing resort to pedagogy: I am the Master and you are the student—submit to me.

So much of the actual material practice of grammar & the rhetoric of grammar is about an exercise of force, regulating who is in and who is out, who has authority to write and speak, and who does not.

Now, if we want to play a gotcha game of cultural authority, I won't end up the student. I mean if we're going to play that kind of priggish game—where to even start? It wouldn't be an exaggeration to imagine that I've spent a good one-third of my waking life reading & writing. That's about ten years, clock time, spent reading. I have a genius IQ. I scored in the top percentile on my SATs—in SEVENTH GRADE. I've had a college reading level since I was 7—gone on to terminal degrees—better call me Dr., Mistah Marbles—have writ big tomes of scholarly research, am accounted an expert in my fields—have taught @ top ten schools—my verse's appeared in print & electronic all over the place, reputable mags—have published articles &c.—

if we want to PLAY that kind of gotcha game—

but I think we both see how obnoxious such displays can be—so let's, please, approach each other as peers or not at all.

& so much of what goes by the name of grammar boils down to exactly that kind of vulgar display— sometimes more & sometimes less subtle.

~

"timeless & eternal classics"

We all remember a first approach @ Shakespeare. We come to it knowing it's supposed to have value—we're told it has value—we want it to have value—to be part of the conversation—& then we get to the text itself and—that stuff is DENSE—At 12 or 13, it's not a thing the timeless value of which is immediately apparent, or easily got at. My point is, being able to apprehend that value takes TRAINING—3 letters, now: J-O-B-S.

Now, I don't dismiss the fact of value, or even what you refer to as "genius"—(though there are some problems with the concept, certainly—it too has a history & context, it's not a transcendent universal essence—see Bob Perelman's "Trouble with Genius")—

Just because I acknowledge the dependence on training our ability to recognize & access the value of a Shakespeare, don't mean I believe just any old thing could have the same effect. It's not that I'm walking you into an empty room in the museum, to trigger the epiphany: "*you* are the work of art."

The point I am making is that new forms of value, literary or otherwise, are often unrecognizable as such. The "grammar" according to which they might be understood as value doesn't yet exist or hasn't yet been acquired.

I've got a very flexible definition of 'avant-garde'—maybe should distinguish from Berger's definition of the historical avant-garde—Dada, Futurist, etc.—shake the words up in a hat & spit 'em out, there's yr poem.

No—I mean as 'avant-garde' those new forms of writing & literary value which are difficult, in their moment, to recognize as such; but which go on to generate & proliferate the grammars by means of which we recognize their value (Dante writing in the vernacular, Shakespeare illiterate of Greek & Latin); by means of which they sometimes come to be confused with value as such, as I feel has happened in yr (& many people's) conception of things—There has always been a cultural police force using the rhetoric of grammar to DENY new articulations of value.

So for me, I have the very weird idea that "literary canon" and "avant-garde" are the same phenomenon viewed from different perspectives of historical distance or nearness; IMPORTANTLY:

that it's just as difficult to recognize the value of 'classical' literary texts as it is to recognize the value of those rare 'avant-garde' works which go on to become the future face of the canon; that many of the same people attempting to forcefully police the boundaries of literary value with recourse to the rhetoric of "timeless classics" & grammar & style, are the very same people who would have decried the vulgarity & unfitness of the classics before they were classical. These people are parasites, basically, leeching off the cultural capital of literary texts without any real understanding of what's at stake.

Now, do I think Wolf Larsen is our next Shakespeare? Not really. I was being a little bit facetious with the 'cultured writers use the word penis all the time' example—but I respect his commitment to self-determination & the integrity of his commitment to the insight that creating NEW value isn't a question of consensus—from a popular readership or a publishing house or the guardians of culture.

~

The point I'm trying to make is: If I say it's a poem, it's a poem.

If I wanted to be more objective, I might say something like, "If it's published as a poem, then, historically speaking, it is a poem. If it is widely circulated enough, and if enough people claim loudly enough that it is or is not a poem, then, historically speaking, it will influence our perception of what is and is not a poem."

And I might go so far as to say that the history of verse is a history of unpoemish innovations that come to be called poetry.

Dickinson was cited early on by Erthona—we like her so well because she created us out of thin air, crafting unpoemish poems that became central to our definition of what a poem is.

For an earlier example, look @ the way print technology shifted the defining onus of poetry from the aural to the visual, how a piece looks and reads and "sounds" on the page. Dickinson, whose poems are very much poems in this sense—literary rather than musical works—could hardly be termed a poet in this earlier, musical sense, dependent as it is on public performance, vocal talent, instrumental training, &c.

The same people who will cry most loudly that this or that is not a poem—as, for example, is so characteristically true of the response of more pedantic readers to some spoken word or hip hop—are the same who would have told Dickinson that her poems weren't poems.

There were, maybe, seagulls.

In my experience—and I acknowledge the following as a personal bias that carries little authority into the realm of the objective or even stereotypical—the people who cry "not poem" have tended towards a certain kind of personality and a certain level of skill.

They have been, by and large, individuals with a degree of literacy—institutional, social, cultural, linguistic and otherwise—but not much imagination. (That's not quite fair—let me at least say, they have not been savants and have had a somewhat restrained sense of vision.)

They have also been, I have found, interested less in the substance of rational discourse than its semblance.

A fact that is, to my mind, self-apparent in the relevant claim: "This is not poetry." This claim tends to be asserted on the basis of a mystical personal authority derived from communion with the universal-historical nature of verse—all while proclaiming itself to be a guardian of objective reason and culture—and is, as far as I can tell, largely impervious to the argumentative force of history, contemporary example, expert opinion, or the dictionary.

Also, I win.

-Lee

A TELEPATHICIST MANIFESTO
Lee Sharks & John Johnson

1. Telepathicism is about having thoughts, telepathically.

2. Telepathicism is NOT a method or style or school or *writing*. Telepaths HATE writing: It's boorish and stupid and boring. Writing is like plowing a field with an old-fashioned cow. Telepaths are like advanced super computers plowing a field with eBay.

3. The telepath is stranded in time. Writing is a cow-plow, but it's what the telepath has to work with.

4. Telepathic writers do not train as writers, diddle sentences, or work with words. Language is a dusty string in the telepath's brain, causing an aneurism.

5. The telepath has a craft, and that craft is mind control powers.

6. Telepaths give birth to luminous tumors made of light. Inside their minds.

7. A telepathic tumor is the hope of the human race.

8. A telepathic tumor's gestation takes 18 sentient lifetimes. All of them are spent in furious thought, giving birth with a grimace of work and fluid. Ash and dirt. Dust and spit.

9. Tiny metropolises of unpaid cyborg researches study literary history for ten thousand years inside a telepath's

brain.

10. A telepath also does not have a brain, in the same way that a telepath does not write.

11. A telepath does not NEED to write, in the same way that a telepath does not need a brain.

12. A telepath has a mind, but just says no to tele-pathways of neurons and sensory dendrites.

13. A telepath exists in a cloud, generally.

14. A telepath exists in THE cloud, specifically.

15. Telepaths practice their craft of mind control powers via controlling minds, not brains or writing.

16. Telepaths also generally and specifically have control of writing and brains, but hate it.

17. Tumors that are the hope of the human race, and cyborgs that are unpaid or woefully underpaid for their level of qualification, make up cogs outside the machine of Telepathicism. They are cogs, and they are not cogs, but neurons, and they are not neurons, but sensory dendrites, and they are not sensory dendrites, they are whole brains, and they are not whole brains, they are writing, except, they are not writing, they are created telepathically and they are tumors and cyborgs and they are the omniscient hope of humanity.

18. Because Telepathicism is about having thoughts, telepathically.

EMOTICONS OF MIDNITE
Lee Sharks

I saw the most educated person on the poetry website
      banned from the poetry website, indignant confused
      and hurt,
trolling the boards at dinnertime deleting his poems and
      comments,
eloquent-fingered typist burning for a historically relevant
      poetry community in the emoticons of midnite
who loneliness and jitters and sullen-faced and sad sat up
      reading in the quotidian emptiness of condominiums
      skittering across the tops of chat rooms
      contemplating literary criticism
who was unable to find employment in the academies
      imagining steady work and purpose among the
      scholars of tenure—

ah, Sigil—while you are not real, I am not real,
and now we're really in the total vegetable soup of time—

BACKLASH: 'THE NEW HUMAN ILLITERATI'

CORNELL HERWITZ, professor and literary historian, published "The New Human Illiterati" in *Partisan Review,* vol. CXIV, No. 4 (Spring 2007). More than twenty years later, in his autobiography *Bad Disciples*, he continued to criticize Lee Sharks, whose "innovations," Herwitz explained, "consisted not in a principled stand in the realms of aesthetics or ethics, but rather in the many years he had envied me, his inability to carve out a niche within the academy, and childish foot-stomping." Herwitz was part of the informal community of New York literary critics and writers associated with Language Writing who passed from radicalism to trite political correctness in their careers after September 11th. In his attack on the hyper-authorialism, self-centeredness, and verbosity of the New Human writers in his 2007 article, Herwitz appointed himself "spokesman of the arrière-garde," as his biographer, Hyde Morten, knew.

The result of Herwitz' article was an influx of letters to the *Partisan Review* defending the New Humans, including one by Rebekah Crane. In the "Correspondence" section of the following issue of the journal, Crane wrote that the New Human writing was "less a reaction than a movement. It is a movement forward, away from, to start with, twenty years of the false binary between the tepid, sterile, unremarkable workshop writing" by writers like "Rita Dove, Billy Collins, and others who were so characteristic of the trends in mainstream 'professional' writing for the past few decades; and 'avant-garde' writers like [Charles] Bernstein, [Ron] Silliman, [Lyn] Hejinian, [Kenneth] Goldsmith" and others who typify "the equally canned, kneejerk post-humanism now three decades past its prime. Put both camps together, and you would be hard-pressed to find ten noteworthy poems."

Herwitz and other academics and commentators continued to cast aspersions on the New Human writers in the pages of *Partisan Review*. For example, in the Fall 2008 issue, Herwitz wrote in "The New Naivety and the Non-Novel" that the "public acclaim afforded Lee Sharks and Jack Feist, whose work combines a warmed-over avant-gardism with a posturing sentimentalism, underscores the fever that has developed on both poles of the cultural divide for anything totalizing, intense, fervid, and new; ten, or even five, years ago the New Human movement would have gone unremarked." In the same issue, French critic Alain Boudreau, reviewing Rebekah Crane's small-press anthology of literary translations, *Day and Night: Conversations with Sapphic Desire*, started by noting, "Rebekah Crane is regarded as the brightest of New York's New Human poets. Since the other possibilities are Lee Sharks, Jack Feist, and Johannes Sigil, no one will contest her preeminence." Boudreau, who had grown close with novelist Tao Lin, wanted Crane to stop "copying Anne Carson and find her own voice. Maybe the New York scene is part of the explanation for her reserve; the startling aspect of the New Human writers is the degree to which they ape tradition. I suppose they think they must be 'postmodern,' and 'postmodern' just means going through the ritual rejection of one's predecessors that has been dated for at least a century. Maybe a concerned friend should discretely explain to Lee Sharks that neither Walt Whitman nor Ezra Pound are so very *avant-garde*."

***

THE NEW HUMAN ILLITERATI
Cornell Herwitz

Lee Sharks' little collection of poems, *Pearl*, which got Telepathicism off to such a furious start just a couple of years ago, bore a dedication to Jack Feist ("secret hero of these poems, who gave off a brazen clangor of brain in eighteen books composed in half as many seconds, inventing a DIY electronic prosody and contemporary eternal epic"), Johannes Sigil ("author of *Tiger Leap*, a total novel which will invent new madnesses for humanity"), and Ichabod Spellings ("author of *All That Lies within Me*, an autobiography composed by the cosmos"). At least for now, humanity has no new madnesses to contend with due to the inability of *Tiger Leap* to locate a capable publisher, and we may never have the opportunity to learn what the cosmos wrote in Spellings' autobiography, but thanks to the Contemporary Classics imprint of Vintage, two of Feist's contemporary eternal epics, *On the Net,* and *Stationary: The American Journals*, have now been unleashed on the world. When *On the Net* appeared last year, Gillian Meriam noted the occasion in the New York *Times* by calling it "a monumental event," likening it to the publication of *On the Road* in the 1950's. But even prior to the novel's actual publication, the rumor circulated that Feist was the figurehead for a new coterie of iconoclasts and visionaries who called themselves the New Humans, and before long his glossy visage (bearded, of course, with an untended garden of thick brown hair spilling over his forehead) was popping up on the internet, he was being avariciously sought out for YouTube interviews, and he was headlining at a Greenwich Village nightclub where, in true East Coast fashion, he read selections of his DIY electronic prosody to an overlay of mixed samplings and dub step.

Although the nightclub act is rumored to have been a flop, *On the Net*'s somewhat kinder fate sent it to the top of the best-seller lists for several weeks, and one needn't look far to see the reasons. Americans love nothing more than representative novels, and what could be more representative in this Age of Facebook than a novel that advocates for the "young generation?" (The minor detail that Feist is in his thirties was very admirably overlooked by fans and sycophants.) More than that, though, I think the advent of the New Humans was looked at with a certain sigh of relief by many who had long been turned off by the infamous intellectualism, difficulty, and polished "professionalism" of the new century's writing. This is what they had been looking for: boisterous, principled, in-your-face youth flipping over the tables in the temple, rather than abstruse, comfortable, well-paid teachers of literature crafting experimental verses with one hand and grading Introduction to English Composition essays with the other. Literary communities are not particularly in vogue nowadays, but the idea of the literary community continues to hold a powerful interest—nowhere more than in the middle class, filled to the seams with college-educated men and women who guiltily think of themselves as Philistines and of intellectualism as the way of the altruist.

As far as appearances go, the intellectualism of *On the Net* is highly appealing. Here is a coterie of fearless young people ghosting across the web (mostly trolling, with a limitless supply of pseudonymous Gmail accounts and usernames), seemingly everywhere at once, injecting their contagious ethos into geographically far-flung cultural movements from the West and East Coasts to London, Berlin, Paris, Dubai, Shanghai—and so on—funded by next-to-nothing (outside of the occasional Kickstarter proposal or ill-gotten NEH grant), typing incessantly about love and God and HUMANS, strung tight on a pharmocopia of nootropics and legal stimulants (but never heavy drugs like LSD or heroin), and collaborating feverishly with likewise hipper-than-thou Americana and neo-folk musicians. From time to time an analytical-critical or seriously theoretical variable enters the equation, but the typical mood attained by Feist is ecstatic:

> We hopped onto a random discussion forum to see what was on the menu. Lee went AFK to reboot his wifi router, and Jo and I scrolled down into a kind of jury-rigged writing workshop. I saw a wild poem, the wildest poem in the world, and turns out the writer is this homebrewed anonymous discussion board virtuoso with no more regular readers than the two or three moderators on this particular forum; you could see his luminous prosody casting waves of light across the entire forum, across the whole dim forest of it that night. The other posters fell down before him. He didn't have a publication to his name and had the utmost regard for everyone. I thought to myself, ZAP, watch that poster write. That's HUMANITY, here I am with HUMANITY. His poem exploded into the forum, calling the mods by name, and they gave the most glowing replies on the net, and I replied with the biggest adoration of all. "Hey you nobody man, that thar poem'll save the world from its own self, that thar poem is the hope of the HUMAN race." And the poem took it in like it was made for it, glowing. It was the spirit of HUMANITY unknown in the same lonely chat room as I was. I wished I could read his whole pure corpus and what the hell he'd been writing all his life besides luminous poems like that. WHAMEE, I said to my soul, and Lee came back and away we went to www.poetry.com

Feist's glee for the anonymous forum poster goes hand-in-hand with his general preparedness to find the origin of every truth and talent in illiterate amateur types and wannabe ESL illiterati. His conception of the life of creative writing at the university is "thousands and thousands ceaselessly whinging for a morsel of recognition amongst themselves... pleading, slavering, obsequious, bowed, all so they could take one of those meaningless pretentious Best Nepotist Prizes," whereas the rest of the world (on the internet) is filled almost completely with overlooked talents of integrity.

for general correspondence
or to collaborate on the Crimson Hexagon

contact lee @
leesharks00@gmail.com

www.ingramcontent.com/pod-product-compliance
Lightning Source LLC
Chambersburg PA
CBHW071001040426
42443CB00007B/606